W9-CPB-780

LIFE CYCLE OF A...

Frog

Revised and Updated

Angela Royston

Heinemann Library
Chicago, Illinois

www.heinemannraintree.com
Visit our website to find out more information about Heinemann-Raintree books.

To order:

☎ Phone 888-454-2279
💻 Visit www.heinemannraintree.com to browse our catalog and order online.

©2001, 2009 Heinemann Library
an imprint of Capstone Global Library, LLC
Chicago, Illinois

Edited by Adrian Vigliano and Diyan Leake
Designed by Kimberly R. Miracle and Tony Miracle
Original illustrations ©Capstone Global Library Limited
   2001, 2009
Illustrated by Alan Fraser
Picture research by Tracy Cummins and Heather Mauldin
Originated by Chroma Graphics (Overseas) Pte. Ltd.
Printed in China by South China Printing Company Ltd.

13 12 11 10 09
10 9 8 7 6 5 4 3 2 1

New edition ISBNs: 978 1 4329 2519 2 (hardcover)
                    978 1 4329 2536 9 (paperback)

The Library of Congress has cataloged the first edition as follows:
Royston, Angela.
  Life cycle of a frog / by Angela Royston.
    p. cm.
  Includes Index.
  Summary: An introduction to the life cycle of a frog from the time it is a tiny egg laid in water until it is two years old.
    ISBN 1-57572-613-0 (lib. Bdg.) –
    ISBN 978-1-57572-536-9 (lib. Bdg.)
    1. Frogs—Life cycles—Juvenile literature. [1. Frogs.]
    I. Title
QL668.E2R656 1998
597.8'9—dc21
                98-39692

Acknowledgments
The author and publishers are grateful to the following for permission to reproduce copyright material: Getty Images pp. 11 (© De Agostini Picture Library/DEA/S. Montawanari), 13 (© Robin Smith), 28 bottom right (© Robin Smith); Natural Science Photos pp. 6 (© Richard Revels); Nature Picture Library pp. 9 (© Warwick Sloss), 28 top right (© Warwick Sloss); Photolibrary pp. 7 (© OSF/G.I. Bernard), 8 (© OSF/Paul Franklin), 10 (© OSF), 12 (© OSF/Paul Franklin), 16 (© OSF/G.I. Bernard), 17 (© OSF/Paul Franklin), 21 (© Paulo De Oliveira), 23 (© Paulo De Oliveira), 24 (© OSF/G.I. Bernard), 25 (© OSF/Terry Heathcote), 29 bottom right (© OSF/Terry Heathcote); Photoshot pp. 14 (© Bruce Coleman/Jane Burton), 15 (© NHPA/G.I. Bernard), 18 (© NHPA/Stephen Dalton), 19 (© NHPA/Stephen Dalton), 29 top right (© NHPA/Stephen Dalton), 20 (© Bruce Coleman/Kim Talyor), 22 (© Bruce Coleman/William S. Paton); Shutterstock pp. 4 (© Tom C. Amon), 5 (© W. Woyke), 29 bottom left (© W Woyke), 26 (© FloridaStock), 27 (© Ttphoto), 28 top left (© WitR), 28 bottom left (© Thomas Mounsey), 29 top left (© Dr Morley Read).

Cover photograph reproduced with permission of Minden Pictures (© Stephen Dalton).

Every effort has been made to contact copyright holders of any material reproduced in this book. Any omissions will be rectified in subsequent printings if notice is given to the publisher.

We would like to thank Michael Bright for his invaluable help in the preparation of this book.

Contents

Some words are shown in bold, **like this**. You can find out what they mean by looking in the glossary.

Meet the Frogs

This is a tree frog.

There are many different kinds of frogs all over the world. Some live in trees. Some live in **swamps**.

1 day	1 week	2 weeks	5 weeks

All frogs live
near water.

Frogs are amphibians. This means
they spend part of their life in water
and part on land. The frog in this
book is a common frog.

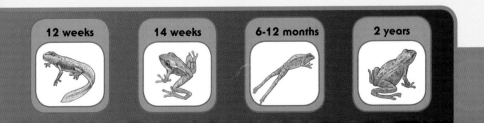

12 weeks

14 weeks

6-12 months

2 years

A Mass of Eggs

These frogs have just laid masses of eggs in a pond.

A frog begins life as a tiny egg laid in water. The egg is part of a clump of eggs called **spawn**.

1 day

1 week

2 weeks

5 weeks

The spawn is like a big blob of slimy jelly. The black dot inside each egg is a tiny **tadpole**.

There may be thousands of frog eggs in a clump of spawn.

12 weeks

14 weeks

6-12 months

2 years

Hatching

The tadpoles grow bigger and bigger.

Fish and other animals eat some of the the **spawn**. Hundreds of the frog eggs keep growing.

1 day

1 week

2 weeks

5 weeks

The baby frogs that hatch from the eggs are called tadpoles.

One day the **tadpoles** push their way out of the eggs. They hang onto the spawn until their tails grow longer and stronger.

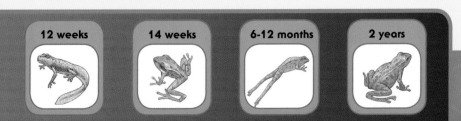

12 weeks   14 weeks   6-12 months   2 years

1–4 Weeks

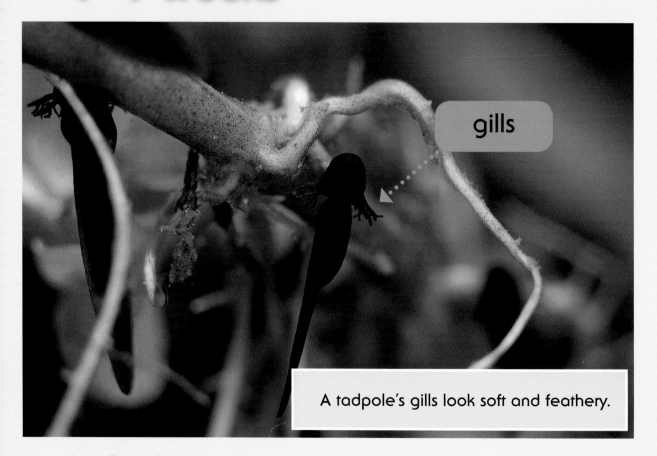

gills

A tadpole's gills look soft and feathery.

Tadpoles have **gills** to take in **oxygen** from the water. Soon the gills will disappear.

1 day

1 week

2 weeks

5 weeks

Tadpoles swim among plants in the water.

Water insects and other animals eat many tadpoles. But the other tadpoles nibble tiny plants and grow bigger and stronger.

12 weeks

14 weeks

6-12 months

2 years

5 Weeks

A tadpole uses its tail to move through the water.

The **tadpole** begins to change into a frog. The back legs grow first.

1 day

1 week

2 weeks

5 weeks

Without **gills**, tadpoles cannot breathe underwater.

Lungs grow inside the tadpole's body. Now the tadpole swims up to the surface of the water to take in **oxygen**.

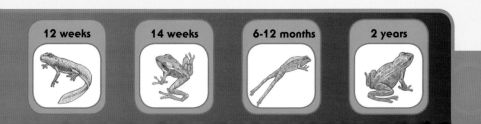

12 weeks

14 weeks

6-12 months

2 years

5–12 Weeks

gill pouch

Front legs grow inside the **tadpole's gill** pouches. The gill pouches start to bulge.

Soon the tadpole's front legs will push through its gill pouches.

1 day

1 week

2 weeks

5 weeks

The tiny animals in this picture are water fleas.

The tadpole still uses her long tail to swim among the plants. She catches water fleas in her wide mouth.

12 weeks

14 weeks

6-12 months

2 years

12 Weeks

The tadpole's tail gets shorter and shorter.

The **tadpole** is almost a froglet. Now she swims by pushing with her long back legs and **webbed feet**.

1 day

1 week

2 weeks

5 weeks

The froglet listens for danger.

The tiny froglet now has no tail. She climbs out of the water onto a leaf and looks around.

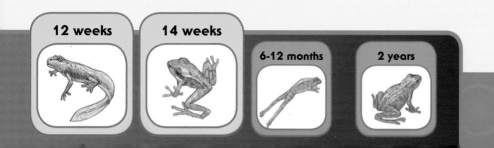

12 weeks 14 weeks 6-12 months 2 years

3 Months

Froglets may climb onto big leaves on the pond.

One day lots of tiny froglets climb out of the pond.

1 day	1 week	2 weeks	5 weeks

This froglet is diving back into a pond to get wet again.

The froglet's skin is very thin. She must be careful not to let it dry out.

12 weeks

14 weeks

6-12 months

2 years

3–6 Months

A frog uses its tongue to catch its food.

The little frog is hungry. She sits very still and waits. Then her long, sticky tongue flicks out, and she catches an insect.

| 1 day | 1 week | 2 weeks | 5 weeks |

Grass snakes eat frogs and other small animals.

The frog hears a grass snake slithering toward her. She croaks and dives quickly into the pond.

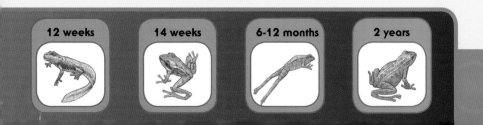

This frog has found a place to spend the winter.

Winter comes and the weather is very cold. The frog looks for a safe hole by the side of the pond. She will stay here and **hibernate**.

1 day	1 week	2 weeks	5 weeks

This frog has caught a butterfly to eat.

One warm spring day, she wakes up, feeling very hungry. She crawls out of the hole and leaps off to find food.

12 weeks

14 weeks

6-12 months

2 years

2 Years

Another year has passed. The frog's body is fat with eggs. **Male** frogs are calling from the pond.

The **female** frog swims towards the male frogs in the pond.

1 day	1 week	2 weeks	5 weeks

A male frog holds on to the female and they **mate**. After a while the eggs leave her body.

A new mass of **spawn** floats away after the frogs mate.

12 weeks

14 weeks

6-12 months

2 years

Pond Life

A frog's life is dangerous. Birds, fish, and many animals feed on **spawn**, **tadpoles**, and frogs. Only a few eggs live to become fully grown frogs.

This heron has caught a frog to eat.

1 day	1 week	2 weeks	5 weeks

Adult frogs return to the pond where they were born.

Some frogs may live for up to 10 years. In the spring, they lay thousands of new eggs in the pond.

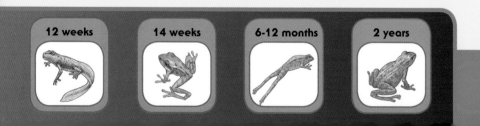

12 weeks

14 weeks

6-12 months

2 years

Life Cycle

Frog spawn

Tadpoles hatch

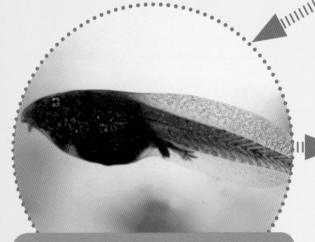

2 weeks

5 weeks

12 weeks

3 months

1 year

2 years

Fact File

- Some frogs can jump nearly 10 feet (3 meters), so they could jump from the foot of your bed to right over your head!

- A frog can breathe through its skin as well as through its mouth.

- When a common frog first leaves the water, it is about the size of your thumbnail.

- The largest frog is the goliath. It lives in Africa. It is large enough to eat small birds and mice.

Glossary

female girl

gills parts of the body some animals have to take oxygen in from water

hibernate rest or sleep all winter

lungs parts of the body some animals have to take oxygen in from air

male boy

mate come together (male and female) to produce young

oxygen gas that living things need to breathe into their bodies to stay alive

spawn mass of frog, toad, or fish eggs

swamp wet, marshy ground

tadpole young frog with a rounded head and a long tail

webbed feet feet that have a layer of skin stretched between the toes

More Books to Read

Hibbert, Clare. *Life Cycles: Life Cycle of a Frog.* Chicago: Raintree, 2005.

Thomson, Ruth. *Learning About Life Cycles: Frog.* New York: PowerKids Press, 2007.

Trumbauer, Lisa. *Life Cycle of a Frog.* Mankato, MN: Capstone Press, 2006.

Index